My Natural Horses

Special thanks to Lisa Huhn (www.equinextion.com), whose generosity and commitment so profoundly changed my life and the lives of so many horses and their people.

Published by
Hug a Horse Farm
775 Cloverville Road
RR2 Stn Main
Antigonish, NS, B2G 2K9
Canada

www.hugahorsefarm.com

Editors: Nancy Rose, Lisa Huhn
Copy Editor: Elizabeth Leighton
Proofreaders: The Watsons

Photo Credits:
Anne Louise MacDonald — cover photos and all photos except for those listed below.
Glynnis Hawe pg 3 (bottom); F. X. MacDonald pg 8-9 (background), pg 29 (left), pg 37 (top and bottom); Nancy Rose pg 48; Dawn Boyer pg 54 (1); Tara Stewart pg 54 (2), pg 56 (6); Trish Lowe pg 54 (3), pg 56 (1), pg 57 (9), pg 58 (2, 6); Katie Rogers pg 54 (4), pg 58 (1, 3); Rebecca Bush pg 55 (5); Becky Moore pg 55 (6), pg 58 (4); Charlotte Blackett pg 55 (7), pg 56 (2), pg 59 (7); Liz Carbine pg 55 (8); Tim Burch pg 55 (9); Tim Kadar pg 55 (10), pg 59 (10); Tammis Pringle pg 56 (4); Nichole Anderson pg 56 (5), pg 59 (8); Marielle Roy pg 57 (7); Diana MacKay pg 57 (8); Kari Bowser pg 57 (10); Judit Klein pg 57 (11); Lisa Huhn pg 57 (12); Jeane Dekter pg 58 (5); Kelly Snowdon pg 59 (9, 11); Helene Benoit pg 59 (12).

Printed and bound by Lightning Source

ISBN 978-0-9813910-0-7

My **Natural Horses**

Anne Louise MacDonald

Isabelle is a seven year old half Friesian, half Thoroughbred. She is 15.3 hands tall (160 cm or 63 inches at the top of her shoulder). Her favorite things are running fast, green grass and learning new tricks.

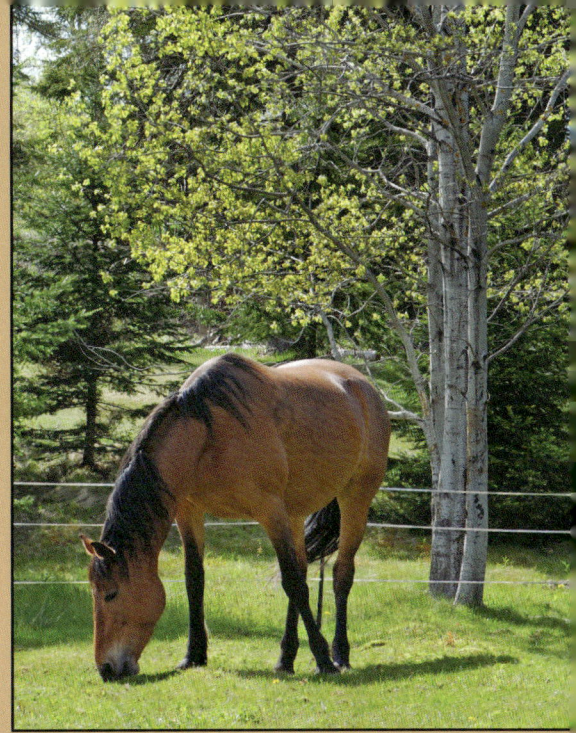

Isabelle is an all-natural horse. She was born and raised in a natural herd in northern Alberta and shipped to me in Nova Scotia when she was one and a half.

At that time, I owned an old horse named Sham. I planned to let him retire when Isabelle was four and mature enough to ride. But Sham died suddenly two days before Isabelle arrived.

Isabelle needed a horse friend, so I went looking for another horse.

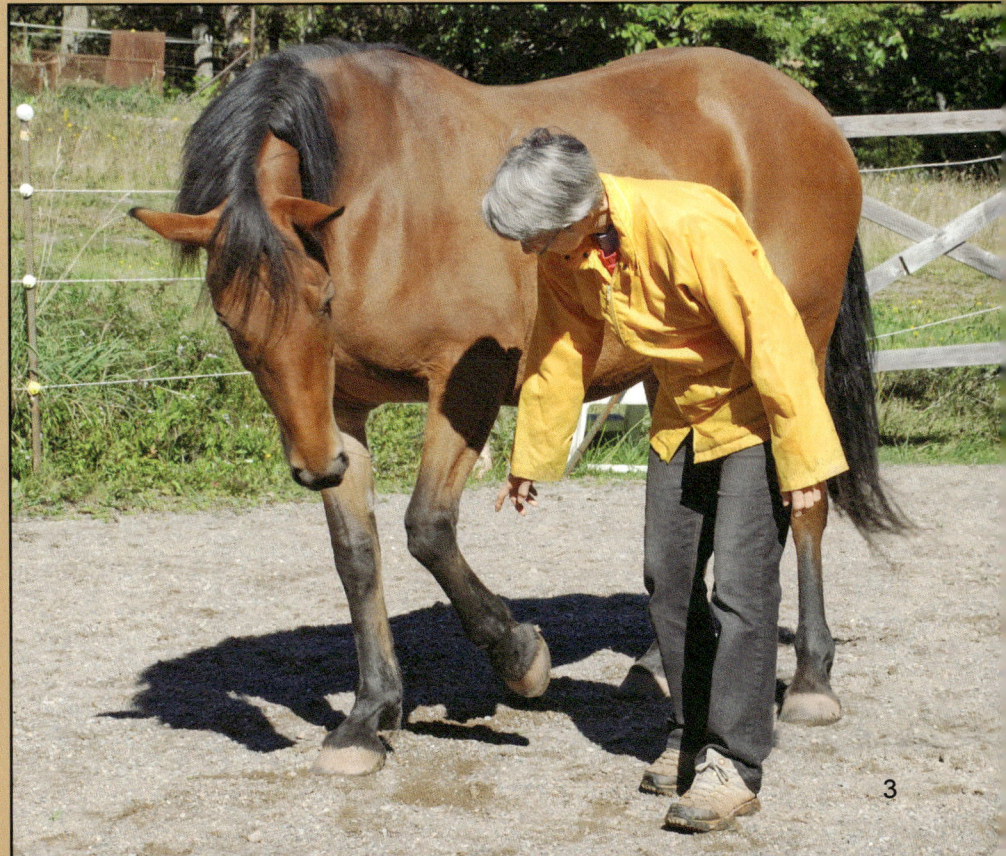

3

Prince is twenty years old. He's a Cheval Canadien, 14.1 hands tall (145cm or 57 inches). His favorite things are food, little girls and standing in the sun.

Prince was born in Quebec, where his breed began in the seventeenth century. There, he was trained for riding and to pull a wagon, a sleigh, and a plow.

He came to Nova Scotia when he was six and belonged to a young girl for nine years.

After I bought him, he missed his girl. Every time we went for a trail ride he would rush in the direction of his old home! It took him almost a year to adjust, but he's happy now. It helped when I started hugging him every day.

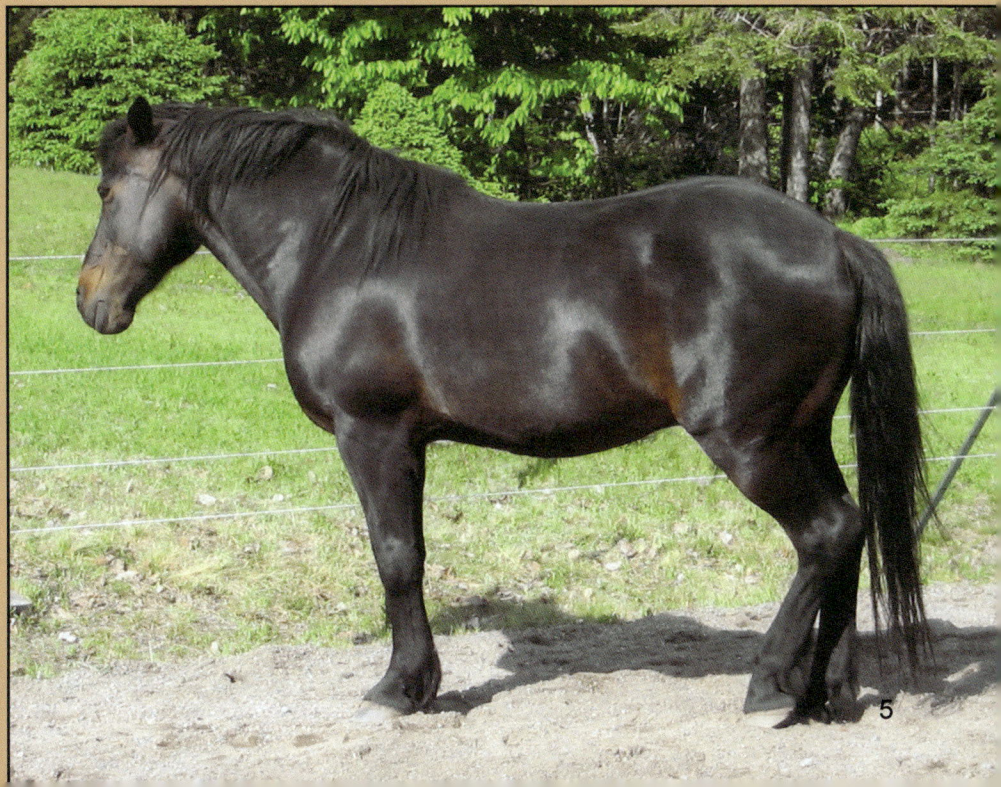

5

And then there's Tummy. He isn't a horse, but he's a goat as big as a pony! He loves thumping with his head, being bossy and anything sweet (unless someone has licked it first).

Tummy was bought as a companion for Sham. I bought a goat instead of a horse because at that time I didn't realize my property had enough room for two horses. Tummy and Sham were very best friends.

Tummy is now ten years old and thinks pushing strangers around is fun. He is really quite sweet and knows how to shake 'hands'. I think he is smarter than most dogs.

This is where they all live. They roam from the shelter, through the brook and along the gravel paths in the forest, or follow the road to the riding ring and the pasture.

They keep busy watching our neighbors and the wildlife (chipmunks, squirrels, groundhogs, beavers, foxes, coyotes, deer, chickadees, eagles and more).

When I arrive, they come to greet me. If Isabelle sees me carrying a halter, she knows we are going to do something fun. Sometimes she gets a firm look on her face and walks quickly away. I just wait. She marches to one of her favorite spots, unloads a poo, and comes right back — ready for action.

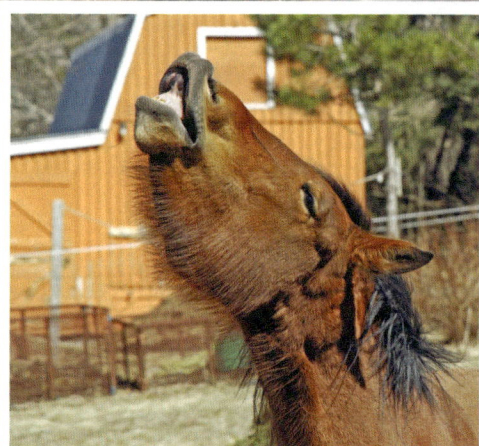

8

SPRING

Spring arrives with brighter evenings and singing birds, but early spring cannot decide whether to be warm and dry, or cold and wet. We can have snow, sleet, rain or hot sun ... all in one day!

As the days get longer, the horses start to shed — even before the snow begins to melt.

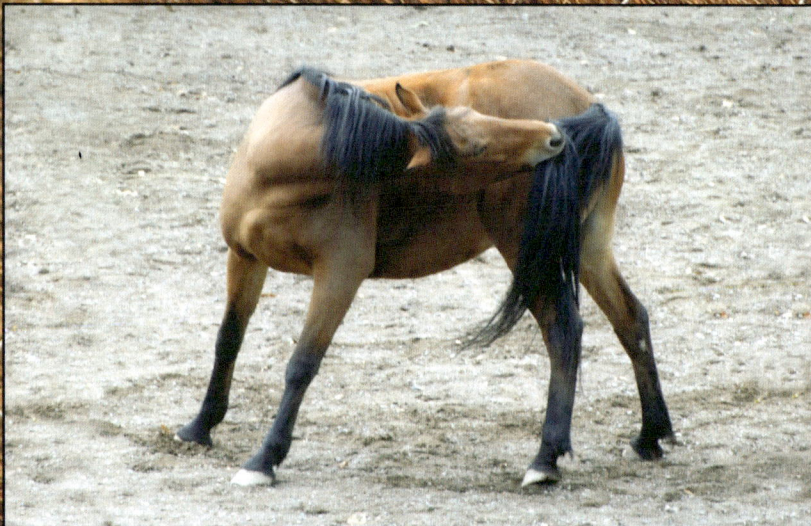

It takes the horses about three months to drop their entire winter coat.

They get busy rubbing and rolling to loosen up the shedding hair.

Natural horses have relaxed, flexible bodies that allow them to get at those hard-to-reach itchy spots.

But it's always nice to have a friend to help.

Or an apple tree.

Isabelle's dark 'underwear' is the last of her warm winter coat to shed and gives her dapples for about a month.

At this time of year, my horses are extra happy to have me brush them. Brushing is a wonderful way to bond with horses.

Friends have exclaimed that I must do a lot of grooming to get my horses so shiny. But I don't have to. They do most of it themselves!

Natural oils and a fine layer of dust and dander next to the skin give my horses a waterproof raincoat.

A light rain just beads on the surface of their coats. In a heavy rain, the coat forms little tufts that shed water like shingles on a roof. The longer hairs on their chins and lower legs funnel water away like rain gutters.

On wet days, the horses like to roll to squeeze off extra water. Then they get up and shake to fluff their coats again.

They can get protection from wind and rain by standing beside the woodshed or one of the piles built from fallen tree branches in the woods. If there's a cold rain for days, they go to the shelter now and then to get completely dry.

15

Spring thaw means soft sand for galloping!

When the melt begins, the paths in the snow turn to solid ice. The horses still **run around**. Living outdoors as the ground changes lets them know exactly where the slippery spots are. But when the ice finally leaves, they let loose with full speed spins, leaps and bucks.

Sand is also perfect for sunbathing and sleeping.

Sometimes the horses sleep in the forest but they like the riding ring better. They feel safer if they can see all around them. Then they go into a dead-to-the-world sleep.

Though natural horses can get several hours of rest standing up, they lie down for deep sleep. This deep sleep may happen in many small doses, as short as five minutes each.

Giving the horses bedding in the shelters is like giving them toilet paper! They will always pee and poop in bedding. Pee-soaked bedding is bad for their feet, so years ago I stopped using bedding.

At first I worried about where they slept at night. But when I found body prints in the sand and 'nests' in the forest — and happy horses every morning — I never worried again.

17

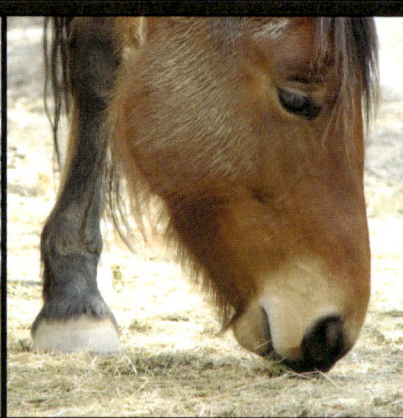

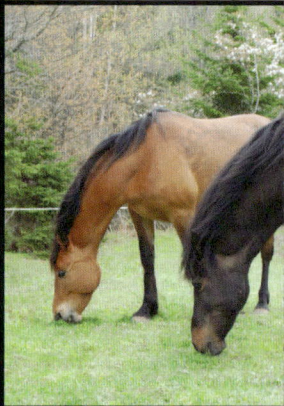

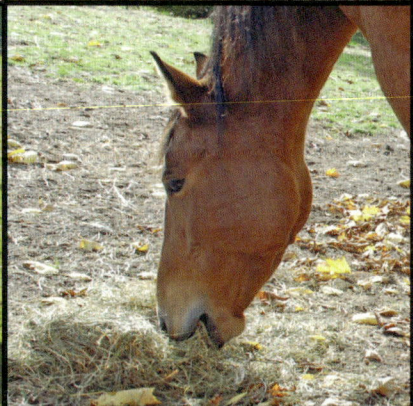

My horses eat for at least sixteen hours every day.

Horses have very small stomachs. They need small amounts of grass or hay available all the time. Wild horses forage, moving long distances each day in search of tasty, nutritious plants. I get my horses to forage by putting clumps of hay by the shelter and in many spots on the graveled forest paths.

The trick is to spread just enough hay so they have to hunt for the last bits, but they never have empty stomachs. If I put out too much hay, the leftovers get stomped and peed on.

The spring sun exposes hay that was buried by ice and snow. This hay ferments and tastes sweet. The horses eat most of it. As the weather gets warmer, I rake the paths to keep them clean and dry.

19

What goes in must come out!

Each horse poops at least fifteen times a day. Because my horses' living area is less than one acre, I pick-a-poo every day. If I didn't, the manure would get mashed into the dirt and become poo-mud. Poo-mud grows bad bacteria that will rot horses' feet.

Also, natural horses do not eat from ground that has poop on it. This keeps them from getting too many internal parasites like worms.

On cool mornings, steam rises from the composting manure. There is very little odor as it turns into rich dark soil.

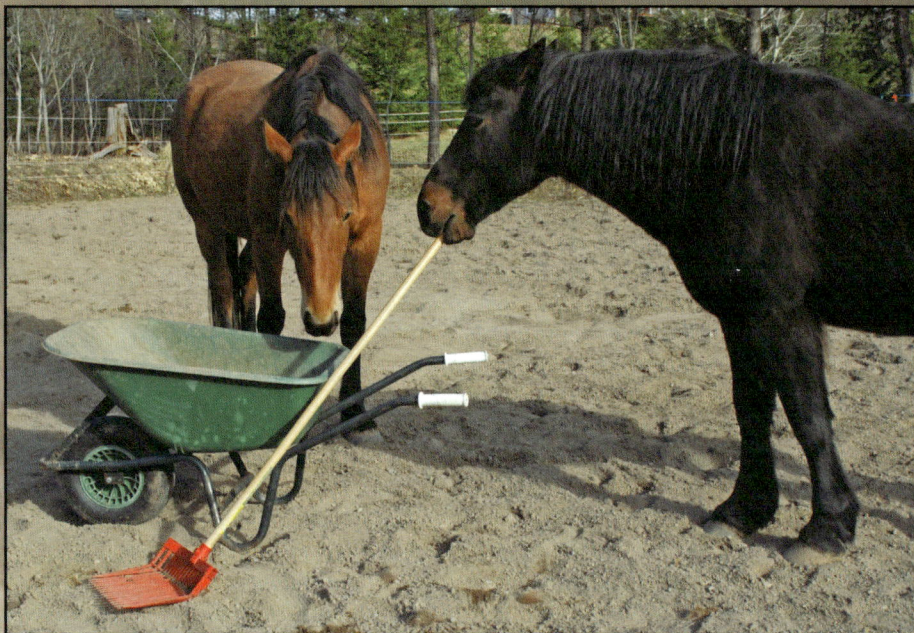

I heap the manure into many little piles. Little piles compost faster than big ones. It only takes one year to be garden-ready.

The horses pretend to help.

Isabelle leaps for joy when the grass starts growing.

Warm spring weather means pesky blackflies.

Every year the very first hatch of flies seems to annoy the horses, but in a day or so they get used to them. Swatting and kicking at flies is good exercise for muscles and joints.

Windy days are great for blowing the flies away.

When the wind is really strong, I put the hay against the branch piles in the forest so it won't get blasted off the property.

SUMMER

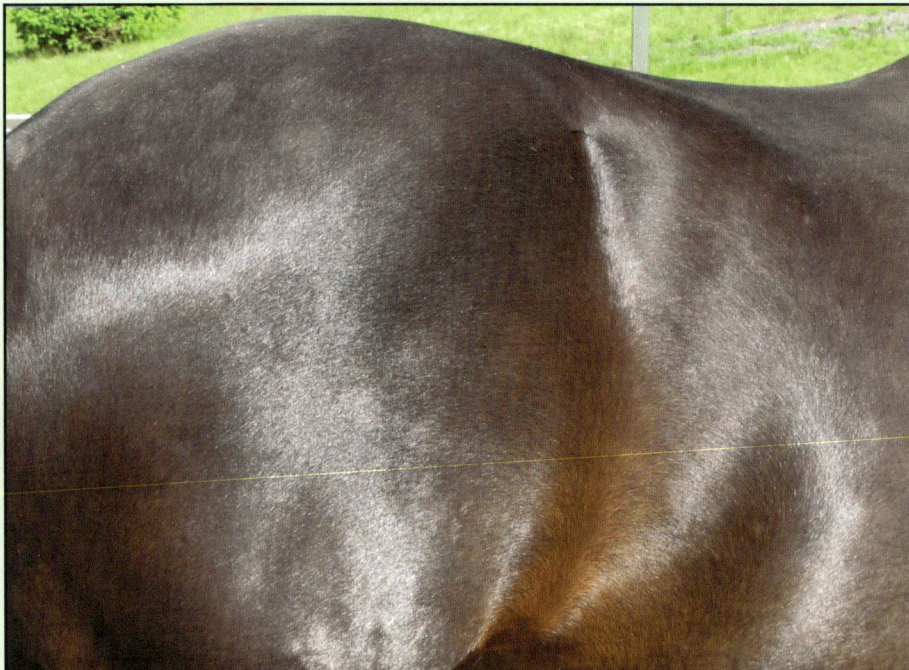

Summer in Nova Scotia is not too hot and not too dry. Early summer brings short silky coats and green everywhere you look.

Even the gravel paths turn green as seeds from the winter's hay sprout in the heat.

The pasture is very small.

I can only let the herd into my pasture to graze one hour a day. Otherwise they would chew the grass down to dirt.

Summer also offers nutritious weeds, leaves, roots and berries which add to the menu of hay, black-oil sunflower seeds and other treats like apples and carrots.

In the shelter, there is always a block of salt and a bucket of minerals. When the weather is very hot, the herd can consume one small salt lick every week.

The horses prefer the running water in the brook to the automatic waterer in the shelter.

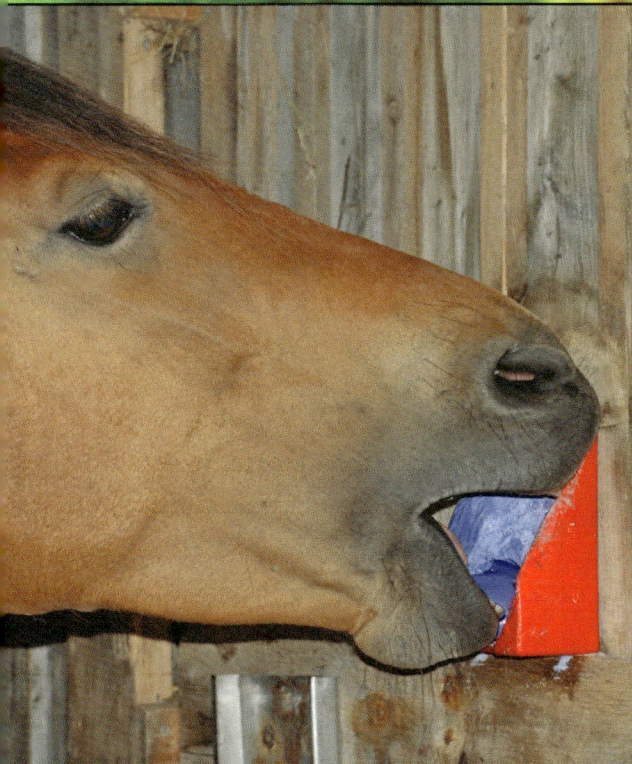

You can't have summer without flies.

They are a normal part of outdoor life and the horses mostly ignore them.

Prince's dark color attracts more flies. Isabelle has learned to stand close and give her flies to him.

The horses' natural diet makes them less tasty to flies.

The *big* biting flies like horseflies are impossible to ignore! When they arrive, the shelter gets used the most.

The shelter is the lean-to on the side of the barn. It is 3 x 7 meters (10 x 23 feet). Horses like a space around them of at least 2½ meters (8 feet). Only friends are allowed in that space. My shelter could fit more horses as long as they were all friends.

Hanging out indoors can be very boring!

But it's cooler inside – the doors at each end catch the smallest breeze. And it's darker. Horseflies don't fly in the dark.

I use fly repellent on the horses when I ride so we can enjoy our time together. It's hard to practice dressage with horseflies biting Isabelle's belly!

Prince doesn't mind flies as much. He's happy to go trail riding any time – except on hot humid days when he would rather sleep in the shade. Me too.

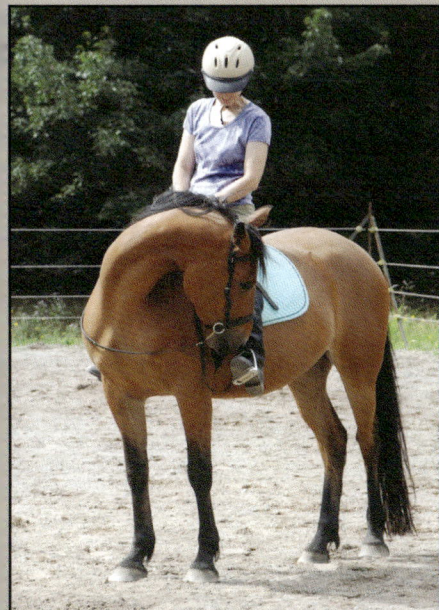

29

Summer rain drips off Isabelle's rump and tickles.

Prince is more concerned about the umbrella over my camera than the water running down his nose. Despite their short summer coats, the rain does not wet the skin.

FALL

Fall brings frosty mornings and no more flies. It begins with forests filled with warm colors and ends with cold browns and grays.

The summer coats start to shed as the days get shorter. By the end of September the horses feel like big plush toys with enough fluff to hide a chickadee's toes.

The second shedding of the year creates more itchies.

Isabelle can almost reach the center of her back. She loves it when Prince scratches it for her.

Scratching each other is called mutual grooming and is done between friends. They start nibbling on the top of the mane and work along the spine to the rump. The nibbling sometimes becomes nipping and they squeal and jump around just for fun.

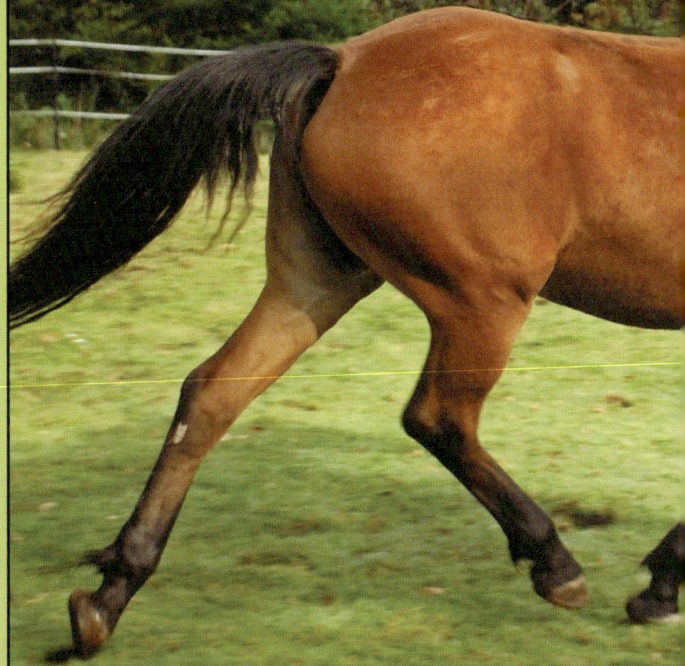

My natural horses eat more food in the fall. It takes extra energy to grow thick winter coats.

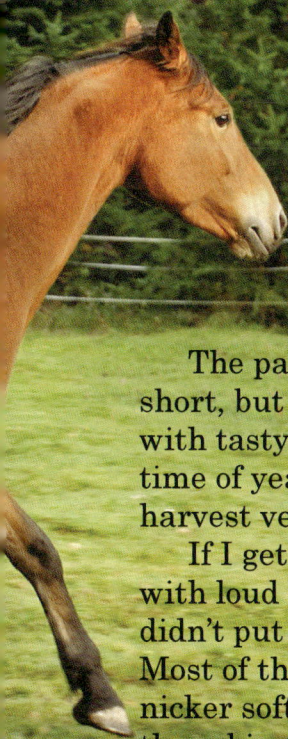

The pasture grass gets very short, but the forest floor fills up with tasty leaves. It's also a good time of year for apples and other harvest vegetables.

If I get greeted in the morning with loud whinnies, I know I didn't put out quite enough hay. Most of the time the horses just nicker softly or quietly stare with those big dark eyes.

35

Fall's fresh air makes frisky horses.

Isabelle loves to run anytime, but Prince prefers cooler weather. Together they gallop as fast as they can through the forest. Running full speed is good for their hearts, muscles and minds.

This is also our favorite time of year for riding. There are no more flies in the woods. Prince adores riding the trails with other horses and ponies.

Isabelle likes to get her feet trimmed outdoors next to a pile of hay with a good view.

This is what Isabelle's natural feet look like. The rubbery parts under the hoof are called the heel bulbs and the frog (top left). They touch the ground and cushion each step just like the heel of a running shoe. In soft ground the frog makes a print shaped like a big piece of pie (top right).

From the side, the front feet (bottom left) and the back feet (bottom right) are shaped like triangles.

If a horse stands with one back foot tipped up on its toe, it usually means the horse is resting. When a front foot is like this, something is wrong.

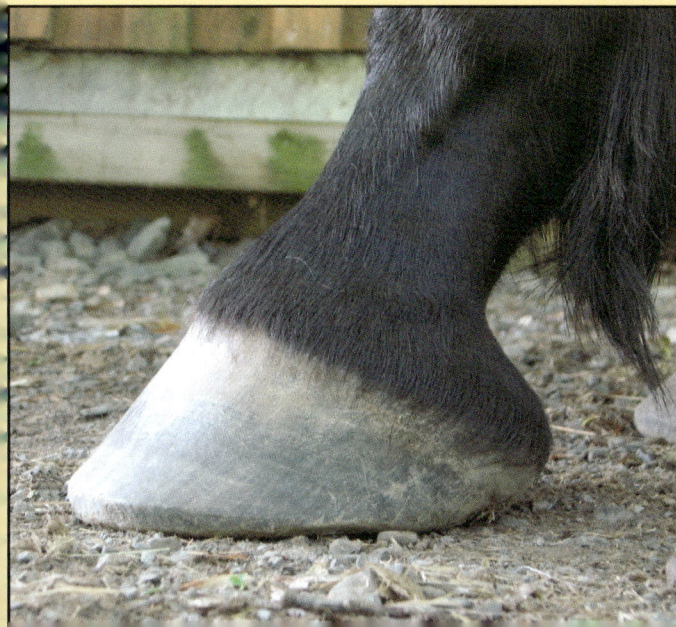

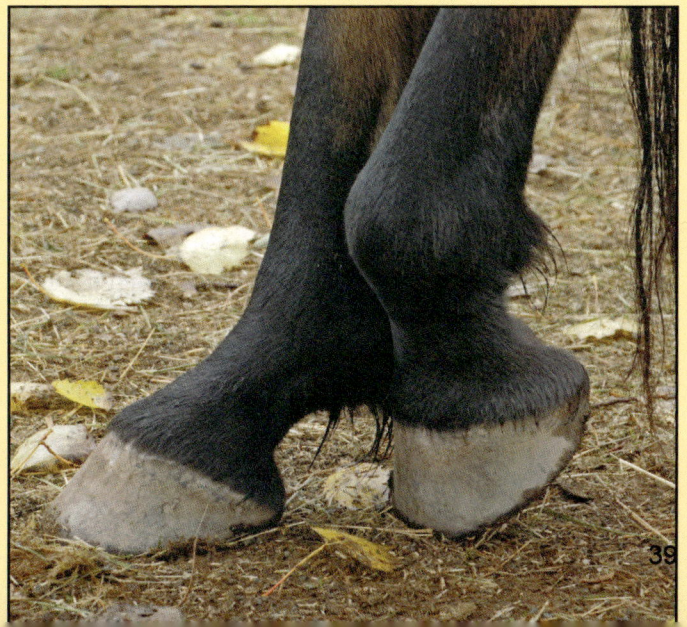

By the end of fall the horses are wearing their winter coats.

The long guard hairs are for shedding water and the thick undercoat of shorter hairs hold warm air against their skin.

As the first snow falls, Isabelle stretches in a big bow. She is relaxed and warm and all ready for winter.

41

WINTER

Winter can be bright sunshine on drifts of snow or gray days of cold rain. The average winter temperature in Nova Scotia is -6°C (20°F) but can go as low as -30°C (-22°F).

No matter what, Prince loves winter. Snow piles up on his thick coat without melting. It even adds insulation and makes him warmer.

A day of freezing drizzle is no reason to go inside.

My horses only got cold one time. A bad ice storm broke a tree across the path to the forest and kept them from eating all of their hay. Hay in the belly is like fuel in a furnace. Empty bellies mean cold horses. It took less than twenty minutes of eating to warm them up again.

44

Sunshine is an excuse to have a snooze.

Sunny days come with colder temperatures but the horses soak up rays and eat less hay.

Goats like to lean on their friends. Prince enjoys resting his head on Tummy.

Isabelle is not so fond of Tummy. She often pretends she is going to bite him. Tummy complains but then runs and hides behind Prince.

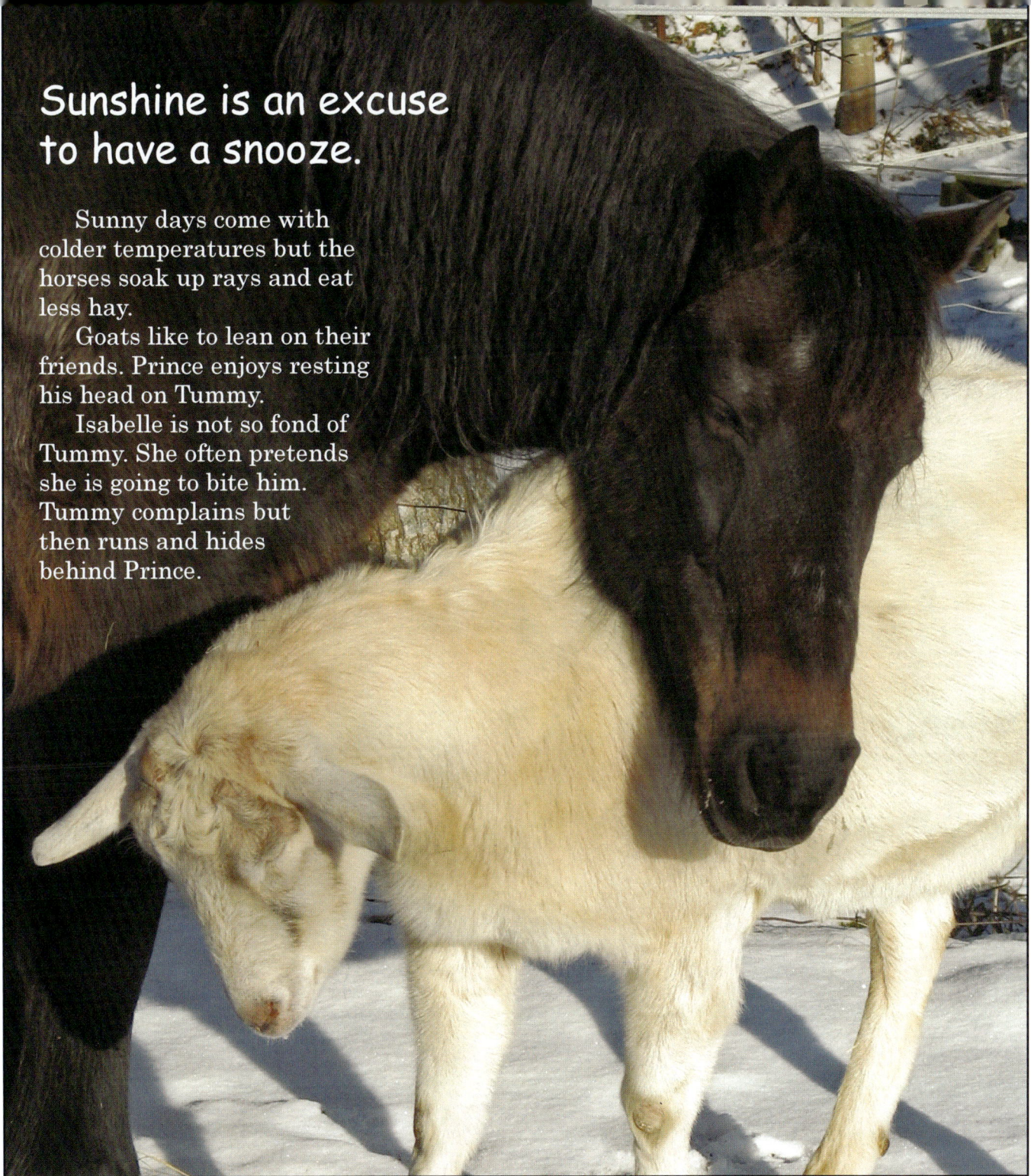

Fresh snow calls for play!

Isabelle teases Prince so he will chase her. Then she dances circles around him. They both buck and kick and run.

When they get sweaty, they roll and shake to dry off.

I put out more hay in colder weather.

The horses go from hay pile to hay pile. The deep snow gives them excellent exercise.

When I bought Prince he was fat. I fed him all the hay he could eat — but spread it around — and he lost weight!

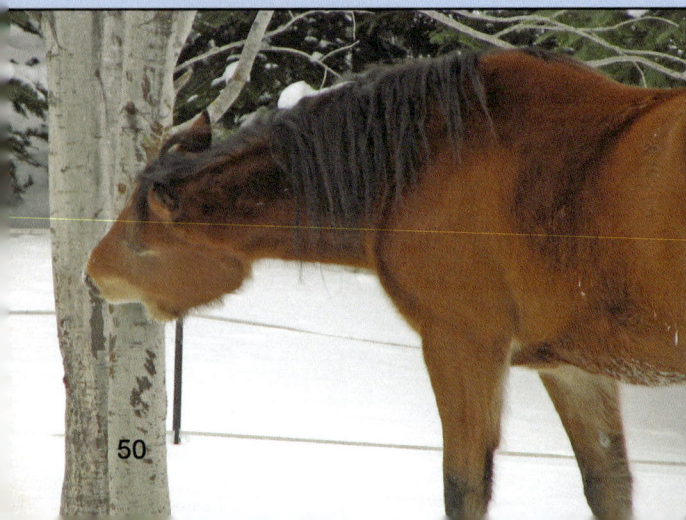

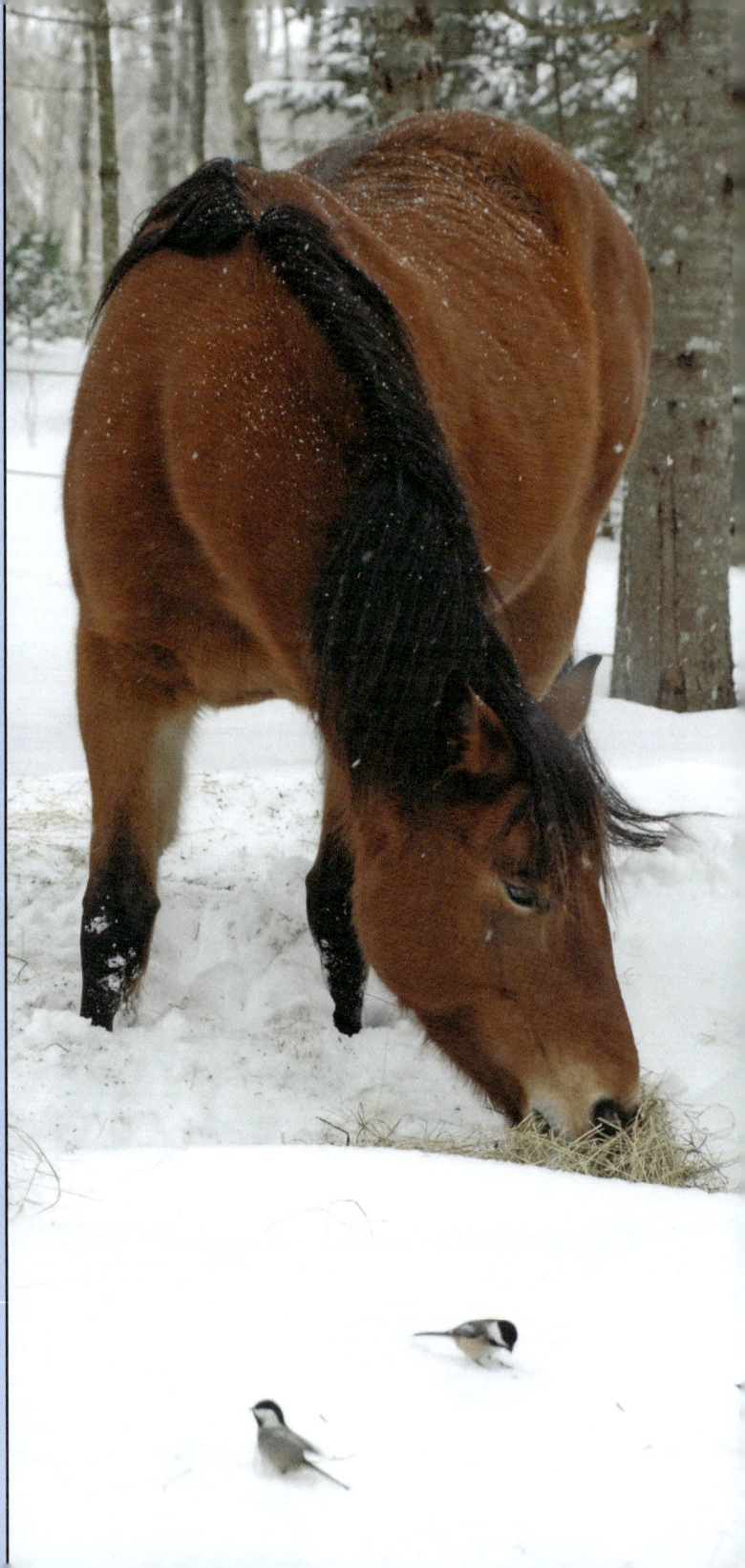

To digest more hay,
the horses drink
more water.

In winter they break the ice in the brook.
They can get some water from eating snow too.
The automatic waterer in the barn has warm water.

Even natural horses can get bored outdoors. Some days
they chew on the wood in the woodshed. They like the old,
soft wood the best. They can make a mess.

Twigs and tree bark are tasty treats.

I also give them extra black oil sunflower seeds. This type
of sunflower seed can be eaten shells and all. They have to
share them with the chickadees.

Now you have seen my natural horses through all four seasons, and how I follow the five F's of Natural Horse Care.

1. Freedom — living outdoors with reasons to move as much as possible
2. Friends — living in a herd (at least one other horse)
3. Food — eating mostly grass, grass hay, and free-choice salt and minerals
4. Footing — living on clean solid ground with at least one soft spot for rolling
5. Feet — having bare hooves trimmed in a natural form

Natural horses are everywhere! Here are a few of them.

(1) Canada — Donius W is a sixte[...] year old Friesian stallion, produc[...] of intelligent, willing and frien[...] offspring with remarkable athle[...] abilities. He is Isabelle's father.

(2) Canada — Kelly and Hadley[...] seven year old part Newfoundla[...] pony. He is smart, curious a[...] playful and he grows the m[...] beautiful winter coat.

(3) Canada — Mike on Skid[...] Skiddy is a twelve year old Quar[...] Horse. She is a big money earner [...] a champion team penning horse [...] Canada and the U.S.

(4) U.S. – (left to right) Ibn, Lu[...] Ike and Smurf. Ibn is a twenty-thr[...] year old Arabian. He loves havi[...] his very own farm to run. Lucy is [...] six year old Quarter Horse. She w[...] a championship in dressage. Ike [...] a two year old half Oldenburg, h[...] Thoroughbred. He loves to zo[...] around the field and thinks h[...] special. Smurf is a fifteen year [...] Quarter Horse, rescued from b[...] treatment. He now trusts his ne[...] owner and will take him anywher[...]

(5) U.S. — Destiny and Elizabe[...] Destiny is a seven year old dra[...]

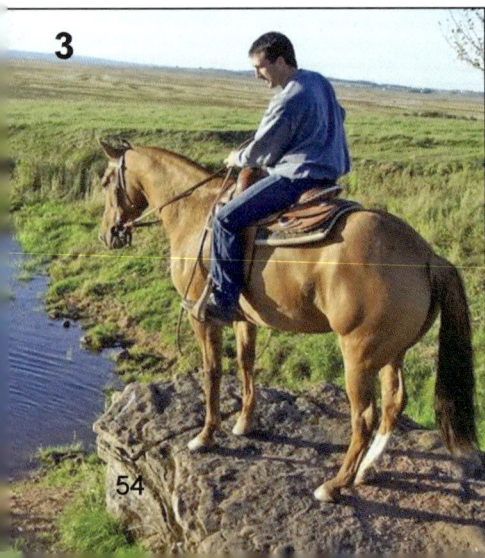

54

oss mare in dressage training.

Canada — Shadow is an eleven
ar old Appaloosa. He is a big flirt
th the girls.

South Africa — Caitlyn on Daz,
four year old half Arabian, half
elsh pony. He lives on a game farm
nong herds of wild impala.

U.S. — Major is a six year old
nnessee Walking Horse who has
en barefoot and natural for over
ree years. He is "healthier and
ore comfortable to ride than ever."

Ireland — (left to right) Kerry,
lly, Elaine and Shona riding Savak,
ry, Donnie and Scottie. Savak is
nine year old Arabian endurance
rse who has done thirty and fifty
le competitive trail rides. Tory is
nineteen year old part Connemara
no's a super game-pony. Donny is a
teen year old purebred Connemara
no loves her rider. Scottie is a
enty year old mixed-breed — a
ly bomb-proof pony who taught
the children how to ride.

0) U.S. — Tess is an eight year
l Oldenburg. Angela is teaching
r dressage but thinks Tess would
ther be an endurance horse.

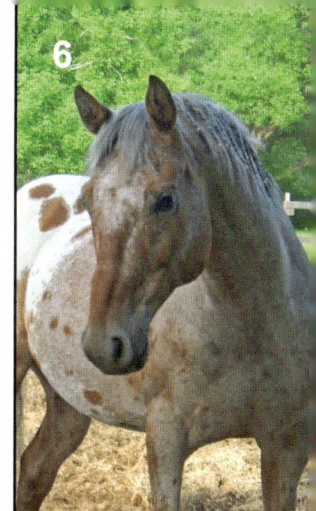

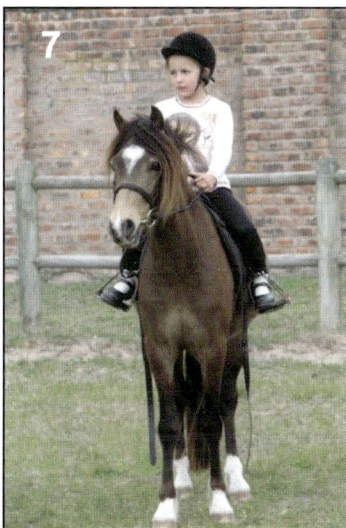

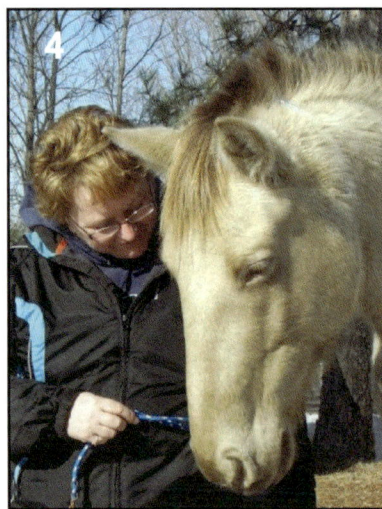

(1) Canada — Kali is an eight ye[ar] old Quarter Horse from milli[on] dollar blood lines. She is trained [in] western reining and trail riding.

(2) South Africa — Christine [on] Forte. Forte is a seven year old o[ff] the-track Thoroughbred. She n[ow] excels at showjumping.

(3) Norway — Kirsti leads Synn[øve] for a ride on Vilja, a six year o[ld] Norwegian Coldblooded Trott[er]. Their Shetland ponies, Gabrie[l] and Spirit, like to tag along.

(4) Canada — Ice is a five year o[ld] Tennessee Walking Horse and Ki[rsti's] Natural Horsemanship partner.

(5) Canada — John and Jas[on] driving Caramel and Benjam[in]. Both horses are Cheval Canadie[n]. Caramel is twenty-one years o[ld] and loves to put everything in h[is] mouth. Benjamin is fifteen years o[ld] and likes to follow his people arou[nd] the field to get attention. He is t[he] spitting image of Prince!

(6) Canada — Panzer and Tayl[an]. Panzer is a twelve year old h[alf] Clydesdale, half Quarter Horse. [He] is a lesson horse and really enj[oys] dressage. Taylan is a five year o[ld] Canadian Sport Horse, who has be[en]

natural since birth. She *loves* to
mp.

Canada — Helene and Toby, an
ght year old American Sport Pony
d "the best pony-power ever."

Canada — Eko is a six year old
andardbred and the herd clown.

Canada — Brent team penning
Max. Max is an eight year old
int and a great cow horse.

)) Canada — Olive is an off-the-
ack Thoroughbred retrained for
essage. When she was bought as a
irteen year old, she was very lame
d grumpy. Two years later, she is a
und, sweet, loving family horse.

) New Zealand — Adrian riding
aasta in her first jousting event.
aasta is a six year old half New
aland Stationbred.

2) Canada — (left to right) Vegas,
t and Rico. Vegas is a five year old
arter Horse. He was so lame for
ree years he was going to be put
wn. After getting Natural Horse
re, he can now run faster than
e whole herd! Jet is a four year old
int and new to the natural life.
co is an all-natural five year old
lf Friesian, half warmblood and
abelle's half brother.

1

2

3

4

5

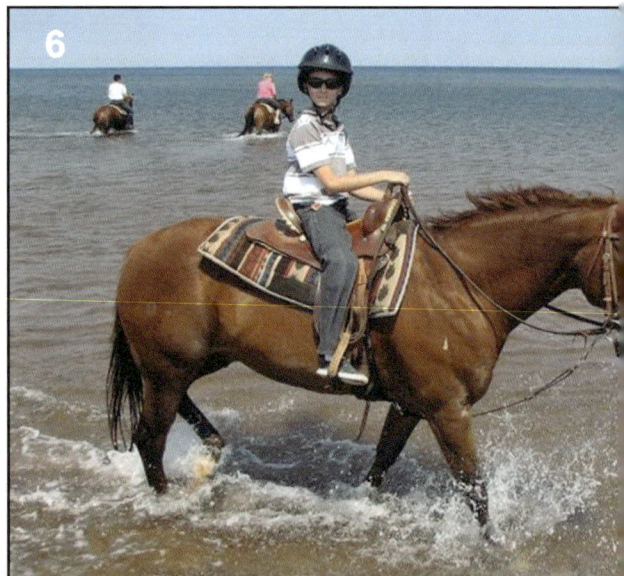

6

(1) U.S. — (left to right) Joe, Maveri[ck]
and Annie. Joe is a twenty year o[ld]
Thoroughbred. He loves jumpi[ng]
and long gallops across open fiel[ds.]
Maverick is a twenty-two year o[ld]
Quarter Horse, a sassy old man w[ith]
tons of energy. Annie is a twelve ye[ar]
old Quarter Horse who acts ditsy b[ut]
is really smart.

(2) Canada — Trish showing Katie[, a]
twelve year old Quarter Horse an[d]
champion team penner.

(3) U.S. — Lisa on Charlie, a twen[ty-]
two year old Thoroughbred, who w[as]
diagnosed with navicular and EPS[M,]
both now cured with Natural Care[.]

(4) Canada — Jazzmon on Ikeda[, a]
twelve year old Arabian.

(5) Australia — Joey is a six ye[ar]
old Welsh Cob, Appaloosa, Quar[ter]
Horse mix. His favourite things a[re]
being ridden bareback and playi[ng]
in the water at the dam.

(6) Canada — Kyle on Dandy. Dan[dy]
is a twenty-three year old Quart[er]
Horse. He has taught three childr[en]
how to ride and taken them all [to]
championships.

(7) South Africa — Christine

uthern Gift. Gift is a six year old oroughbred who loves to jump.

Canada — Beauty and Bear. auty is a ten year old half Morab, lf Paint. She enjoys trail riding. ar is a Standardbred who loves to ld his tail high and show off even ough he is over twenty years old.

Canada — Bella is a four month l Dutch Warmblood. She is very eet and adores being scratched.

0) U.S. — Angela and Izzy. Izzy a thirteen year old Hanoverian. zy was supposed to be put down cause of breathing problems and vicular. After she started living refoot and natural she won the egionals in dressage!

1) Canada — Willow on Smiley, fectionately known as "Safety miley", a nine year old Clydesdale, ddlebred, Appaloosa mix. He has ne eventing, cattle penning and ail riding — all barefoot! He is a ry sensible and brave boy.

2) Canada — Marille and Matthew. atthew is a fourteen year old aflinger and a superb carriage iving teacher.

Sometimes getting
serious photos
of horses is
not easy.

61

LaVergne, TN USA
16 March 2010
176152LV00001B